954   Ganeri, Anita,
             1961-

            India.

$18.60

DATE			

COUNTRY TOPICS

INDIA

Anita Ganeri and Rachel Wright

Illustrated by John Shackell

FRANKLIN WATTS

NEW YORK • CHICAGO • LONDON • TORONTO • SYDNEY

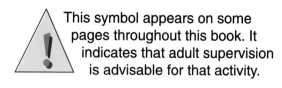 This symbol appears on some pages throughout this book. It indicates that adult supervision is advisable for that activity.

Franklin Watts
A Division of Grolier Publishing
Sherman Turnpike
Danbury, CT 06816

10 9 8 7 6 5 4 3 2 1

Library of Congress Cataloging-in-Publication Data

Ganeri, Anita, 1961 -
India / by Anita Ganeri and Rachel Wright.
p. cm. -- (Country topics for craft projects)
Includes index.
ISBN 0-531-14314-7
1. India--Social life and customs--Juvenile literature.
I. India--Social life and customs--Juvenile literature.
I. Wright, Rachel. II. Title. III. Series.
DS421.G18 1984
954--dc20

Editor: Hazel Poole
Designer: Sally Boothroyd
Photography: Peter Millard
Artwork: John Shackell
Picture research: Veneta Bullen

Printed in the United Kingdom

CONTENTS

Introducing India

NAMASTE! Hello and welcome to India! Before you begin your journey, here are a few facts and figures about India to help you on your way.

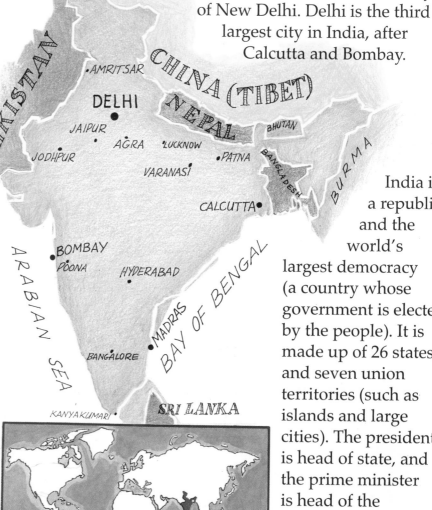

THE INDIAN FLAG

The Indian flag has three horizontal stripes in orange, white, and green. There is a dark blue wheel in the middle of the white stripe. Each part of the flag has a special meaning. The orange stripe represents the Hindus of India, the green stripe the Muslims, and the white stripe the hope that the two can live in peace. The wheel is an ancient Buddhist symbol. It stands for peaceful change. The flag was adopted in 1947, when India gained its independence from the British (see pages 28–29).

INDIA IN THE WORLD

India is the largest country in South Asia and the seventh biggest country in the world. It is shaped roughly like a triangle and covers an area of some 1,266,595 square miles (3,288,000 square km). This includes the tiny Andaman and Nicobar Islands and the Lakshadweep Islands in the Indian Ocean. There is coastline down two sides of the triangle. On land, India has borders with Pakistan, Nepal, China, Bhutan, Bangladesh, and Burma. Delhi is the capital of India. It is divided into two parts – the ancient city of Old Delhi, and the modern city of New Delhi. Delhi is the third largest city in India, after Calcutta and Bombay.

India is a republic and the world's largest democracy (a country whose government is elected by the people). It is made up of 26 states, and seven union territories (such as islands and large cities). The president is head of state, and the prime minister is head of the government. The government buildings are in New Delhi.

NATIONAL SYMBOLS

The peacock is the national bird of India. But the national emblem of India is the four-lion capital (sculpture) of King Asoka. It dates from the third century B.C. It originally stood on top of a tall pillar, which Asoka had built in honor of the Buddha. Each part of the capital symbolizes the teachings of the Buddha. Below the capital there is a motto in Sanskrit, the ancient language of India. It says, "Truth alone triumphs."

The Indian national anthem is *Jana-gana-mana* which means "Thou art the ruler of the minds of all people." It was composed by the poet Rabindranath Tagore, who won the Nobel Prize for Literature in 1913.

MONEY AND STAMPS

The Indian currency is called the *rupee*, written as R or Rs. One *rupee* is divided into 100 *paisa* (p). Coins and bills show the lion capital emblem, and the Hindi name for India, *Bhaarat*. The notes give their value in several different Indian scripts (see below). The word *Bhaarat* also appears on Indian stamps.

THE LANGUAGES OF INDIA

The words in the "Say it in" boxes throughout this book are in Hindi, India's main language. But India has 15 official languages, including English, and hundreds of local dialects. Different languages use different alphabets. Hindi is written in the Devanagri alphabet. The letters in a word are linked by a line running across the top.

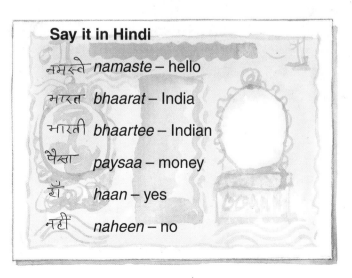

Say it in Hindi

नमस्ते	*namaste*	– hello
भारत	*bhaarat*	– India
भारती	*bhaartee*	– Indian
पैसा	*paysaa*	– money
हाँ	*haan*	– yes
नहीं	*naheen*	– no

Around India

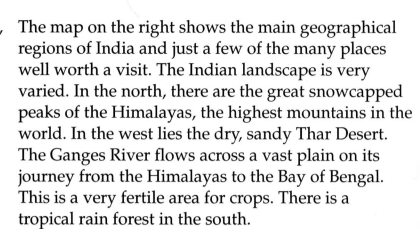

India is such a huge country, and there are so many places to visit and amazing sights to see, that you won't know what to do first! There are high mountains, sandy deserts, and palm-fringed beaches. There are also many ancient buildings, temples, and monuments to explore.

THE RED FORT

The Red Fort, or *Lal Qila*, in Delhi was built by Shah Jahan in 1638. The fort has huge, red sandstone walls over 98 feet (30 meters) high in places. You can have a guided tour of the buildings inside the fort, or enjoy a sound and light show in the evening.

INDIAN GEOGRAPHY

The map on the right shows the main geographical regions of India and just a few of the many places well worth a visit. The Indian landscape is very varied. In the north, there are the great snowcapped peaks of the Himalayas, the highest mountains in the world. In the west lies the dry, sandy Thar Desert. The Ganges River flows across a vast plain on its journey from the Himalayas to the Bay of Bengal. This is a very fertile area for crops. There is a tropical rain forest in the south.

TAJ MAHAL

The Taj Mahal overlooks the Yamuna River in Agra. It was also built by the Mughal emperor, Shah Jahan, in memory of his dead wife, Mumtaz. Shah Jahan wanted it to be the most beautiful building ever seen. He hired architects and craftsmen from all over the world. Work began in 1632 and lasted for 20 years. The Taj Mahal is built of white marble, inlaid with semiprecious stones.

MONSOON

Most of India has three seasons – hot, wet, and cool. They are caused by the monsoon winds that blow in off the Indian Ocean, bringing the rain needed for growing farmers' crops. The hot season begins in March. The wet season begins with the arrival of the monsoon in June. The cool season begins in October. This is the best time of year to visit India.

SHORE TEMPLES

Beautiful stone temples line the shore at Mahabalipuram, near Madras in South India. They were built around the seventh century A.D. and are dedicated to the Hindu gods, Vishnu and Shiva. South India is famous for its temples. Some have very brightly painted gateways.

THE GOLDEN TEMPLE

The Golden Temple in Amritsar is the holiest shrine of the Sikh religion. The temple has been destroyed and rebuilt several times. In 1802, it was given a copper roof that shines like gold in the sun. The temple is surrounded by a lake.

THE PALACE OF WINDS

The Palace of Winds in Jaipur is really a screen made of pink sandstone, with rows of carved windows and balconies. It was built in 1799. At that time, the ladies of the royal court could sit behind the screen and watch the world go by, without being seen themselves.

Say it in Hindi

पहाड़ *pahaar* – mountain

नदी *nadee* – river

बरसात *barsaat* – monsoon, wet season

सूरज *sooraj* – sun

महल *mahal* – palace

Food and Drink

There are Indian restaurants all over the world and Indian food has become very popular. Indian dishes are very tasty. They can also be very hot and spicy, so choose carefully!

A HINDU MEAL

A typical Hindu vegetarian meal consists of several small dishes of spicy vegetables, *dhal* (like thick lentil soup), pickles, poppadums, and rice or bread. More rice is grown in the south so more is eaten there. Wheat is grown in northern India and made into different types of flat bread, such as *chapattis* and *naans*. Yogurt *(dahi)* is another important part of a meal. It helps to cool down your mouth if you have eaten something hot and spicy!

People eat off metal trays called *thalis*, with each dish in a small metal bowl, or off banana leaves. They eat with their fingers. But they only use their right hands because their left hands are thought to be unclean.

FOOD AROUND INDIA

In India, what you eat depends on where you live and on your religious beliefs. Many Hindus are vegetarians – they do not believe in killing things to eat. Some do eat chicken and fish if they live along the coast, but Hindus never eat beef. They consider cows to be sacred animals. Muslims eat chicken (tandoori chicken is a famous Muslim dish) and lamb, but they will not eat pork.

After a meal, people chew *paan* to help them digest their food. This is a mixture of betel nut, spices, and lime paste wrapped up in a triangular betel nut. It turns your teeth red if you eat too much!

GOING SHOPPING

Indian people shop for fresh vegetables, fruit, and other ingredients at the market. There are large indoor markets in the big towns and cities, and small local markets or rows of wayside stalls in the villages. There are also market stalls piled high with colorful spices, flowers for offering at the temple, and tasty take-out snacks.

AND, TO DRINK

With a meal, people usually drink water or a refreshing yogurt drink called *lassi*. This can be sweet (flavored with sugar) or sour (flavored with salt). But the favorite Indian drink is hot, sweet, milky tea. After all, more tea is grown in India than anywhere else!

If you have a sweet tooth, there are plenty of Indian sweets to choose from. Some are sticky and syrupy, such as *jalebi* or *gulab jamun*. Others are made from milk or cream cheese, such as *roshgullas* or *sondesh*. Sweets are often given as gifts on special occasions, such as weddings, or as thank-you presents.

Shopping list

दूध	*doodh*	– milk
मिर्च	*mirch*	– chili pepper
रोटी	*rotee*	– bread (chapatti)
आलू	*aloo*	– potato
गोभी	*gobee*	– cauliflower
आम	*aam*	– mango
चावल	*chaawal*	– rice
सब्ज़ी	*sabzee*	– vegetables

Curry and Spice

Indian cooks like to season their foods with a variety of spices. Some of these spices have a very delicate flavor. Others are so red-hot they can make your eyes water! The measurements of the spices listed in the recipe below will give you a very mild curry.

Potato and Cauliflower Curry is especially tasty when served with rice, chapattis, or any other type of Indian bread. If you decide to serve bread, you can use it to scoop up your curry.

To feed two hungry people . . .

YOU WILL NEED:

LARGE, HEAVY SAUCEPAN

MEDIUM-SIZED SAUCEPAN

5 TABLESPOONS OF COOKING OIL

SMALL BOWL

SIEVE

4 Fl.oz. (120 ml) OR ½ CUP

SERVING DISH

LONG-HANDLED WOODEN SPOON

1 MEDIUM-SIZED CAULIFLOWER

2 MEDIUM-SIZED POTATOES

SHARP KNIFE

CUTTING BOARD

A HANDFUL OF FRESH CORIANDER OR PARSLEY

2 HEAPING TEASPOONS OF TOMATO PUREE

1 TEASPOON OF CURRY POWDER

½ TEASPOON OF CUMIN SEEDS

¼ TEASPOON OF CHILI POWDER

1 TEASPOON OF TURMERIC POWDER

1 TEASPOON OF SALT

½ TEASPOON OF BLACK MUSTARD SEEDS

1. Wash and peel the potatoes and cut them into 1-inch (2.5-cm) cubes.

2. Partly fill the medium-sized saucepan with water. Bring the water to a boil on a medium-high heat. When the water boils, carefully add the potatoes and cook them for five minutes.

3. While the potatoes are cooking, wash and chop the cauliflow into small florets and throw away any thick stalks. When the potatoes are ready, drain them in the strainer.

4. Heat the oil in the large saucepan over a medium heat.

5. Mix the chili powder, curry powder, cumin seeds, salt, turmeric powder, and black mustard seeds in the small bowl.

6. Pour the spice mixture into the saucepan, add the tomato purée, and stir. (Stand far back as you stir. Some of the seeds may pop out of the pan.) Now add the potatoes and cauliflower and cook for about three minutes, stirring continuously. If the mixture starts to burn, turn the heat down.

7. Add 4 oz (120 ml) water to the saucepan, turn up the heat, and bring the water to a boil.

8. Lower the heat, and let the curry simmer gently for about 15 minutes. Stir occasionally.

9. Meanwhile, wash and chop the coriander or parsley into tiny pieces.

10. When your curry is cooked, spoon it into the serving dish, sprinkle the chopped coriander or parsley on top, and serve it hot.

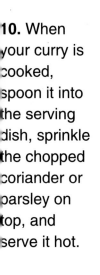

Life in India

About 880 million people live in India, more than in any other country except for China. And the population is still growing. Despite the fact that many people are very poor, Indian life is full of color and bustle, a real mixture of modern and traditional.

WHERE PEOPLE LIVE

More than two-thirds of Indian people live in the thousands of villages dotted all over India. Most people work on the land. They do not own large farms; but many own or even rent small pieces of land. Here they grow food for their families, with perhaps a little extra to sell at the market. It is a hard life. People live in simple houses, sometimes built around open-air courtyards. Each village also has a well and a temple or mosque.

Some people leave their villages and travel to the big cities in search of work. Some get jobs as household servants, hotel workers, or rickshaw drivers. But many return empty-handed. Indian cities are very overcrowded. Many people live in slums on the outskirts of the city. Some cannot even afford to do this. They sleep on the pavement. There are also gangs of beggars, trying to scrape together enough money to live on. Wealthy people usually live in large apartments. They have servants to cook, clean, and keep house for them.

EXTENDED FAMILIES

If you lived in India, you'd probably have not only your parents, but your grandparents, aunts, uncles, and cousins living with you. When an Indian girl gets married, she leaves her family and goes to live with her husband's family. Indian weddings are very elaborate affairs, lasting for several days. The bride wears a special, embroidered sari with beautiful jewelry and elaborate makeup.

Going To School

Indian children are supposed to go to school from the ages of 6 to 14. But children from poor families often leave school early or never go at all. Their families need them to work and help earn money. Apart from ordinary schools, there are also religious schools and schools that teach practical skills such as farming or health care. Village schools are often held out in the open. The children sit on the ground and write on slates, or in the sandy soil.

Indian News

Each year, over 27,000 newspapers and magazines are published in India. They are printed in many different languages. The most famous English-language newspapers are the *Statesman* and the *Times of India*. Many of the most popular glossy magazines are filled with stories and gossip about India's movie stars.

Say it in Hindi

गाँव	*gaamw*	– village
शहर	*shahar*	– city
घर	*ghar*	– home; house
किसान	*kisaan*	– farmer
परिवार	*pariwaar*	– family
स्कूल	*skool*	– school
अध्यापक	*adhyaapak*	– teacher
कूआँ	*kuaam*	– well
अखबार	*akbaar*	– newspaper
किताब	*kitaab*	– book

Putting on a Sari

1. Put on the slip and T-shirt. Wrap one end of the fabric around your waist to form half a skirt and tuck the edge into the waistband of your slip.

2. Pick up the other end of the fabric and pull it around the back of your waist . . .

YOU WILL NEED:

A SHORT SLEEVED T-SHIRT

A LONG SLIP

A LENGTH OF MATERIAL ABOUT 4 x 1 YA

3. . . . across your chest . . .

4. . . . and up over your shoulder. The loose end of the fabric should drape down your back to your knees.

5. Hold out the middle section of the fabric as shown.

6. Fold the loose fabric like a fan until the "skirt" fits you. Tuck the tops of the folds into your slip's waistband. The folds should face the same way as the shoulder covered by the loose end of your sari.

7. Check that the hem at the bottom of your sari is even, and straighten the fabric draped over your shoulder.

Sports and Leisure

Indian people work hard but they also find time to enjoy themselves. Playing and watching cricket, going to the movies, and story-telling are popular Indian pastimes.

SPORTS

Many Indians are cricket crazy. The national teams are closely followed and their performances, good and bad, much discussed! Kite-flying, *kabaddi* (see below), polo, and chess are all traditional Indian sports.

INDIAN DANCE

Kathakali is an ancient, traditional style of Indian dance from South India. Only men are allowed to dance the main roles. They wear elaborate masks and costumes, with brightly painted faces. They dance stories from Indian myths and legends.

MOVIE-GOING

Which city do you think makes the most feature films? Hollywood? Wrong! The answer is Bombay in India. Studios there make about 700 action-packed feature films each year. There are hundreds of movie houses all over India, and traveling movie vans that visit remote villages. And just to show how popular Indian movies are, some 9 million movie tickets are sold every day!

KABADDI

This popular Indian game is a bit like team wrestling. One player has to run into the other team's territory, touch as many of his or her opponents as possible, and then race back to his or her own side without being captured by those that were touched. Now comes the tricky part. All of this has to be done in just one breath! If the player manages to make it back to base in a single breath, all those that were touched are out. To show that the player hasn't taken a sneaky second breath, he or she has to keep repeating the word "kabaddi."

Say it in Hindi

खेल *khayl* – game, sport

शतरंज *shatranj* – chess

पतंग *patang* – kite

नाच *naach* – dance

संगीत *sangeet* – music

बाजा *baajaa* – musical instrument

Indian Religions

Religion plays an important part in the lives of Indian people. Many different religions are followed. People may be Hindus, Muslims, Sikhs, Jains, Buddhists, or Christians. The main religion of India is Hinduism.

HINDUISM

About 8 out of 10 Indians are Hindus. They believe in a supreme being, called Brahman. This being is represented by three main gods – Brahma (the creator), Vishnu (the preserver), and Shiva (the destroyer). But there are thousands of other minor gods and goddesses. They include the elephant-headed god, Ganesh, and the monkey god, Hanuman. Hindus believe that when they die they are born again. Their aim is to break free of this cycle of birth and rebirth. If you lead a good life, you are more likely to do this than if you are bad.

Hindus worship the gods in many different ways. Some people visit a temple and bring offerings of flowers and sweets. Others have small shrines at home where the family worships. Some Hindus don't worship at all – it's not compulsory!

Varanasi on the Ganges River is the holiest city for Hindus. They travel there from all over India to bathe in the river. This is believed to help them break free of the cycle of rebirth.

The Caste System

Hindu society is traditionally divided into four castes (or classes). These were based on the types of jobs people did long ago. The highest caste is that of the *Brahmans,* or priests. Next come the *Kshatriyas,* the soldiers and noblemen. They are followed by the *Vaisyas,* the merchants and traders, and the *Sudras,* the craftsmen and servants. People normally marry others of the same caste, but that is not always the case today.

Followers of Islam

About a tenth of Indians are Muslims who follow the religion of Islam. They worship in buildings called mosques and have to pray every day. Muslims believe in one God, called Allah, and in his prophet, Muhammad. India's neighbors, Pakistan and Bangladesh, are both mainly Muslim countries.

Other Faiths

There are also about 16 million Christians, 12 million Sikhs, 5 million Buddhists, and 3 million Jains in India. The Sikh religion was founded in the Punjab in the fifteenth century by a holy man called Guru Nanak. Sikhs worship in temples, called gurdwaras. Their most important temple is the Golden Temple in Amritsar (see page 7). The Jain and Buddhist religions were both founded around 500 B.C. One of the most sacred Buddhist sites is Sarnath in North India. This is where Buddha preached his first sermon.

Say it in Hindi

मसजिद *masjid* – mosque

साधू *saadhu* – Hindu holy man

मंदिर *mandeer* – temple

देवता *dayvtaa* – god, deity

पूजा *poojaa* – Hindu worship/prayers

बन्दर *bandar* – monkey

हाथी *haatee* – elephant

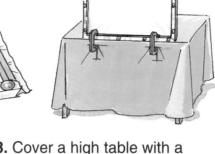

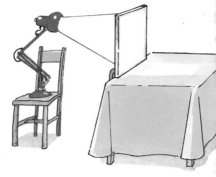

2. Cut out a piece of sheet, big enough to cover one side of your frame. Gently stretch the sheet over the frame and pin it on opposite sides with the thumbtacks. Stretch the sheet again and pin the two remaining sides.

3. Cover a high table with a tablecloth and secure your screen to it with the "G" clamps. The tablecloth will hide your body when you sit behind the screen. Your audience will sit on the other side of the screen to watch the play.

4. Ask an adult to help you set up the reading lamp behind your screen. The lamp should be higher than your head will be when you are sitting down, to keep your shadow from appearing on the screen.

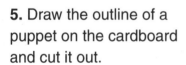

To make the shadow puppets

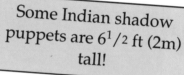

Some Indian shadow puppets are $6^1/2$ ft (2m) tall!

5. Draw the outline of a puppet on the cardboard and cut it out.

6. Using the hole punch or needle, make slits and holes in your puppet to suggest eyes, costume, and jewelry. When the light shines on these holes, they will show through as white. If you want to create color effects, stick some colored cellophane over the cuts.

7. Tape a garden rod to the back of your puppet with tape so that you can move the puppet from below. Then make more puppets in the same way.

. Stand a mirror in front of
our screen as shown, and
urn on the reading lamp. Now
y pressing your puppets
gainst the screen and then
olding them farther away. If
ou look in the mirror as you
o this, you'll be able to see
he different types of shadows
ou are making.

ian shadow puppets are
ually made from leather.
ome have no joints and
cast black and white
hadows onto the screen.
thers have movable arms
nd legs and cast colored
shadows instead. The
leather used to make
olored shadow puppets is
scraped very thin and is
dyed different colors.

9. When you've seen what your puppets' shadows can do,
invent a play for them to perform. Cut out some cardboard
scenery and tape it onto your screen. (Don't forget to remove
the mirror when you stage your play in front of an audience.)

Getting Around

Indian people love to travel. They make long journeys to visit relatives and attend weddings, and pilgrimages to special temples and other sacred places. The big cities are always full of noise and traffic, as people travel to work and to school. Many traffic jams are caused by cows wandering into the road. Because they are sacred, you are not supposed to rush them!

RAIL JOURNEYS

India has one of the biggest railroad systems in the world. And one of the most frequented! The railroads carry some 3.6 billion passengers a year. Many of the locomotives are still powered by steam.

BY BUS

Buses and coaches are usually packed so full, people have to sit on the roof or hang onto the sides. Many of the tourist coaches have air conditioning.

RICKSHAW POWER

Rickshaws can weave easily in and out of even the busiest traffic. Today they are pulled along by people riding bicycles or motor scooters. They used to be pulled along by hand.

INDIAN AIRLINES

Air India is the national airline of India and there are four international airports in Delhi, Bombay, Calcutta, and Madras. Indian Airlines carries passengers on internal flights. There is also a private internal airline, Vayur.

CAMEL RIDING

The best way to travel in the desert is on the back of a camel. Take a cushion – it can be a bumpy ride. In some places camels are used to bring banking services to people.

Say it in Hindi

ऊँट	oomt	camel
गाड़ी	gaaree	car
डाकिया	daakiyaa	postman
रिक्सा	rikshaa	rickshaw
स्टेशन	stayshun	station

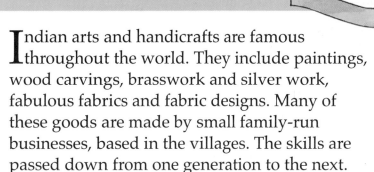

Arts and Crafts

Indian arts and handicrafts are famous throughout the world. They include paintings, wood carvings, brasswork and silver work, fabulous fabrics and fabric designs. Many of these goods are made by small family-run businesses, based in the villages. The skills are passed down from one generation to the next.

MUGHAL MINIATURES

Miniature painting became popular from about the fourteenth century and was used to decorate religious works. The most beautiful paintings were done by artists working for the Rajput princes of Rajasthan. This style of painting flourished in the Mughal court in the sixteenth and seventeenth centuries.

FABRIC DESIGN

India is one of the world's top producers of cotton and silk. Each region of India has a special way of dyeing and decorating the cloth. In Varanasi, gold and silver thread are woven into silk. Saris made from this material are often worn at weddings.

The speciality of Gujarat and Rajasthan is mirror work. Tiny mirrors are sewn into cotton cloth for decoration. Tie-dye designs are also very popular (see pages 25–7).

Papier-Mâché and Carpets

Kashmir is famous for its papier-mâché work. You can buy boxes, letter holders, cups, trays, anything you like. Kashmir is also where the best Indian carpets are made. They are woven from wool or silk, and are very expensive.

Wood Carving

Statues of the Hindu gods and goddesses are often carved from sandalwood, which has a pleasant, natural smell. The craftsmen carve very fine details into the wood – it takes a steady hand.

Jewels of India

Indian women like to wear lots of jewelry – bangles, earrings, necklaces, ankle chains, and so on. Jewelry is usually made from gold or silver, with precious or semi-precious stones. Extra-special jewelry is worn for weddings.

Say it in Hindi

तस्वीर	*tasweer* – picture
चित्र	*chitra* – picture
दरज़ी	*darzee* – tailor
साड़ी	*saaree* – sari
सन्दूक	*sandook* – box
लकड़ी	*lakree* – wood
जवाहर	*jawaahar* – jewel

Tie-dye

Tie-dye is one of the easiest ways of turning a boring white fabric into a jazzy patterned one. Parts of the fabric are knotted or tied so that when the whole piece of cloth is dyed, the tied parts remain the color of the fabric while the rest becomes the color of the dye. This produces an unusual pattern when the ties are undone.

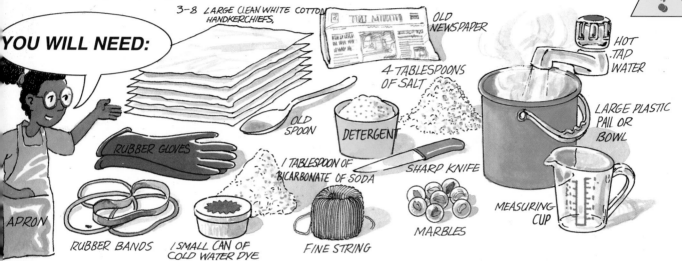

YOU WILL NEED:

3-8 LARGE CLEAN WHITE COTTON HANDKERCHIEFS,
OLD NEWSPAPER
HOT TAP WATER
4 TABLESPOONS OF SALT
OLD SPOON
DETERGENT
LARGE PLASTIC PAIL OR BOWL
RUBBER GLOVES
1 TABLESPOON OF BICARBONATE OF SODA
SHARP KNIFE
MEASURING CUP
APRON
RUBBER BANDS
1 SMALL CAN OF COLD WATER DYE
FINE STRING
MARBLES

(IF YOU WANT TO CREATE MULTICOLORED PATTERNS, YOU WILL NEED A SECOND TIN OF DYE IN ANOTHER COLOR, AND TWICE AS MUCH SALT AND SODA.)

1. To create a spotted pattern, twist some marbles into one of the handkerchiefs and hold them in place with the rubber bands. Twist and tie as tightly as you can to keep the dye from seeping into the tied parts of the cloth.

2. To create stripes, pleat the second handkerchief lengthwise and tie it tightly at intervals.

3. Fold, knot, or bind the remaining handkerchiefs in other ways to create different patterns. Remember that the tied parts will resist the dye, and so form your pattern.

4. Pour enough cold water into the pail or bowl to cover all the handkerchiefs.

5. Spread some newspaper over any surfaces that might get splashed with fabric dye. Then put on the rubber gloves and apron and carefully open a box of fabric dye.

6. Dissolve the fabric dye in 1 pint of hot water and pour the solution into the pail

7. Put the soda and salt into the measuring cup and dissolve in 1 pint ($\frac{1}{2}$ liter) of hot water.

8. Pour the soda and salt solution into the pail and stir well.

9. Wet the handkerchiefs, put them into the pail and stir continually for 10 minutes. Then stir at intervals for 50 minutes, making sure that you keep the handkerchiefs submerged. (If you find it hard to tie them tightly, try leaving the handkerchiefs in the fabric dye for only 30 minutes.)

10. Remove the handkerchiefs from the pail and rinse them under the cold water faucet until the water runs clear. Then wash them in hot water and detergent and rinse well.

11. Untie the bindings and dry the handkerchiefs away from sunlight and direct heat.

You'll need to wash the handkerchiefs separately for the first few washes to get rid of any remaining fabric dye.

To create multicolored patterns, you can add more bindings after step 9, and then go back to step 5 and dye your handkerchiefs a different color. Or you can untie your first bindings after step 9 and retie them in different places before dyeing them with a second color.

This pattern was produced by twisting marbles into the fabric, dyeing it red, removing the marbles, and redyeing the fabric in yellow.

To create this pattern, the fabric was pleated and tied as shown in step 2, and dyed red. The outer bindings were then undone and the whole piece was redyed yellow.

This pattern was produced by binding the center of the fabric and dyeing the whole piece yellow. Once dry, this binding was undone and the center of the fabric was squeezed and held in place by a rubber band. The four corners of the fabric were then tied with rubber bands and the whole piece was dyed green.

Indian History

India is an ancient country with a long and colorful history. It has attracted explorers and traders for centuries, many of whom stayed to rule the country. Here are some of the many key events and characters in Indian history.

THE MUGHAL EMPIRE

In the sixteenth century, India was conquered by the Mughals, a group of Muslims who invaded from the northwest. They ruled over a huge empire, and were responsible for many of India's finest paintings, buildings, and gardens. The Mughals had their capital at Agra. Their greatest emperor, Akbar, built a new city for himself to the west of Agra. It was called Fatehpur Sikri. But the city was abandoned after just fourteen years because of problems with its water supply.

THE INDUS VALLEY CIVILIZATION

The first great civilization in India flourished along the banks of the Indus River in 2,500 B.C. (This area is now part of Pakistan.) It had highly organized cities at Mohenjo Daro and Harappa. Each house had a bathroom and the cities had very good drainage systems. Lots of artifacts have been dug up on the sites of the cities. Among them were hundreds of carved stone seals which were used to stamp a merchant's mark on his goods.

ASOKA MAURYA

King Asoka Maurya came to the throne in 269 B.C. and was one of India's greatest rulers. His empire covered most of India. In 260 B.C., Asoka decided to become a Buddhist and follow the Buddha's belief in peace and nonviolence. Asoka had just waged a successful but bloody war and was filled with remorse for all the people his troops had killed. Asoka built the lion capital which is now India's national emblem (see page 5).

THE BRITISH RAJ

By 1756, Mughal power was in decline and the British were ready to take control of India. They had come to India to trade but had gradually strengthened their power and position. In 1876, Queen Victoria was proclaimed Empress of India. India remained part of the British Empire until its independence in 1947.

INDIAN INDEPENDENCE

At the end of the nineteenth century, a group of young, educated Indians founded the Indian National Congress. Its aim was to campaign for a greater say for Indians in how they ran their country. The British agreed to many of their requests, but also broke their promises. The "Quit India" campaign grew stronger after World War II, and in 1947 the last Viceroy of India, Lord Mountbatten, presided over India's independence. Jawaharlal Nehru became the country's first prime minister.

MAHATMA GANDHI

Mohandas Gandhi was one of the most important campaigners for India's independence. He became known as "Mahatma" which means "great soul." He believed in non-violent, passive resistance. This meant that people marched in protest against the British but were asked not to use violence even if they were attacked.

Say it in Hindi

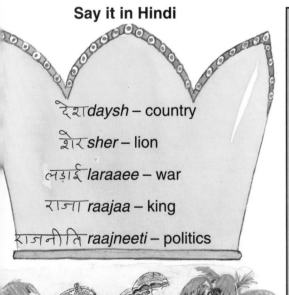

देश *daysh* – country

शेर *sher* – lion

लड़ाई *laraaee* – war

राजा *raajaa* – king

राजनीति *raajneeti* – politics

TIME BAND
2,500 B.C. Indus Valley Civilization
1,500 B.C. The Aryans begin to invade
c563 B.C. Birth of Buddha
269–231 B.C. Reign of King Asoka
320 A.D. Founding of the Gupta Empire in India
1001 Muslim raids in the northwest
1498 Vasco Da Gama from Portugal sails to India, opening up a trade route from Europe
1526 The Mughal Empire begins
1784 The British take control of India
1857 The First War of Independence (Indian Mutiny)
1876 Queen Victoria is proclaimed Empress of India
1885 The Indian National Congress is founded
1947 India gains independence but is divided into Hindu India and Muslim Pakistan
1950 India becomes a republic

Picture Pairs

Play Picture Pairs and see how many of the Hindi words in this book you actually remember! The instructions given here are for two to four players, but as your Hindi vocabulary increases, you might like to make more cards and include more players.

YOU WILL NEED:

OLD MAGAZINES

WRAPPING PAPER

METAL RULER

GLUE

SCISSORS

STIFF PAPER

THICK CARDBOARD

CUTTING BOARD

PAINTS OR CRAYONS

PENCIL

CRAFT KNIFE

To make the cards

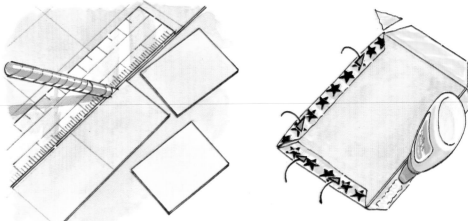

1. Draw 50 rectangles c the same size onto the cardboard and carefully cut them out using the craft knife.

2. Draw another 50 rectangles onto the wrapping paper and cut them out too. These rectangles should be about 1 inch (2 cm) longer and wider than the cardboard ones.

3. Cut the the corners of the paper rectangles as shown and glue them onto your cards.

4. Draw 25 rectangles, slightly smaller than your cards onto the stiff paper and cut them out.

5. Choose 25 Hindi words from this book and write them down with their English translations. (Keep this list beside you as you play the game.)

6. Look through the magazines and cut out any photographs which illustrate the words you have chosen. If you can't find suitable pictures, cut out some more rectangles from stiff paper and paint pictures of your words on them.

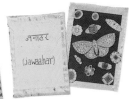

7. Stick each photograph or picture onto the front of one of your cards. Glue the stiff paper rectangles onto the rest of the deck and write a Indian word from your list on each one.

To play the game
The object of Picture Pairs is to collect pairs of cards made up of words and their matching picture.

Each player starts the game with seven cards. The rest of the deck is placed face-down on the table. If you have any pairs, put them on the table in front of you.

Then ask one of the other players if he/she has a card that you need to make a pair. If that player has the card requested, he/she must hand it over and you win the pair and have another turn. If he/she does not have the card, you take a card from the deck in the middle and the turn passes to the next person.

All word cards must be translated into English. If you cannot remember the translation of the word, look it up and miss your next turn.

The player who pairs all his/her cards first is the winner.

Index

Additional Photographs:
DAS 5, 13, 18, 28, Cover; Hulton Deutsch 29; Hutchison 9, 12, 15, 22, 23; Image 4; Robert Harding 6, 8, 16, 17, 23, 24, 28; Werner Forman Archive 6, 23; Zefa 6, 7, 12, 15, 16, 24.